Slow
Work
through
Sand

Winner

of the

Iowa Poetry

Prize

Slow
Work
through
Sand

Poems by Leslie Ullman

University of Iowa Press Ψ Iowa City

University of Iowa Press,
Iowa City 52242
Copyright © 1998
by Leslie Ullman
All rights reserved
Printed in the
United States of America
Design by Richard Hendel
http://www.uiowa.edu/~uipress

Library of Congress
Cataloging-in-Publication Data
Ullman, Leslie.
    Slow work through sand: poems / by
Leslie Ullman.
        p.   cm.—(The Iowa poetry prize)
    ISBN 0-87745-615-1 (paper)
    I. Title.   II. Series.
PS3571.L57S57   1998
811'.54—dc21   97-33396
98 99 00 01 02 P 5 4 3 2 1

Contents

Acknowledgments

Grateful acknowledgment is made to the following publications in which some of these poems, many in earlier versions, first appeared:

American Voice: "Why She Reached" (under the title "Courage"); *Bloomsbury Review*: "Chant," "Sea Opal"; *Blue Mesa Review*: "My Father on the Dock," "This Summer Comes like a Catherine Wheel"; *Crazyhorse*: "Lightning"; *the eleventh Muse*: "In the Very Beginning," "Passage," "Prayer"; *From the Dark Forest*: "Calypso," "Notes on an Island, Wisconsin"; *Green Mountains Review*: "Rose Quartz"; *Gulf Coast Magazine*: "Feathers," "Tonight the Moon"; *High Plains Literary Review*: "At the Estate Auction" (under the title "Garnet"); *Kenyon Review*: "One Side Writes to the Other"; *Lilt*: "Sea Opal," "Slow Work through Sand"; *Pequod*: "Night Trade," "Onyx"; *Poetry Magazine*: "Amethyst," "Aquamarine," "Calypso, Twilight," "Estrogen," "French," "Lent," "Mauve," "Museo de Oro," "Running Horse"; *Prairie Schooner*: "Ambition"; *Puerto Del Sol*: "Cruising"; *Rio Grande Review*: "Lapis Lazuli"; *Texas Poetry Anthology*: "Gourd"; *The Tiguas: Pueblo Indians of Texas* by Bill Wright: "Gourd."

I wish also to thank the National Endowment for the Arts for its assistance and encouragement.

Slow
Work
through
Sand

The Way Animals Are

Sometimes I'm startled to find myself
in this white skin, this blankness,
time's drawings erased
the way highways have levelled
the land's natural drift.
I'm distracted by the history of rain
in a single cactus. I wonder
how heavy the mountain is.
Sometimes I feel the earth tilt
on a great magnet while I sleep
and a man with a history of his own
leaves his wife's body parts in boxes
all over town, while a building is blown up
in another state and 20 children die,
now 30, now 95, not just children, some
still missing, and the numbers
flash across the world in slender cables.

Yesterday I walked the border bridge
into Juarez, where time had stopped — women,
children, begging or selling candy,
their bare feet tough as roots
and their skin streaked with weather.
Such patience in their faces —
the shadow of the Andes,
broad cheek and burnished braid,
rain over terraced slopes,

the breath of childbirth and sorrow
keening through bamboo. Across the river
the windows of my city gleamed.

I stepped into a cathedral
where matrons one by one knelt
by the altar, their privacy
a brief and deepening well,
to speak with someone I wish
I could love. Or fear. Then they rose
and returned to their used bodies,
vessels shaped to gentle fullness,
broken and mended again and again.

Across the blowing litter
of Avenida Juarez, an old man
sat on a curb playing a violin —
a tuneless song that fed
on its own exhaustion.
Once he stopped and put his head
in his hands. Traffic rushed
between us. My eyes touched him
but I didn't cross the street.
This morning he is slow rain
passing through me, waking in the same
grey clothes, tightening his bow

and still I try to sing
in any language I can,
sing to you one at a time
which is all I can do;
there's a slow tongue that some days
runs through me unbidden,
in rhythms I am part of
the way animals are, even when
they're standing still.

My parents were married the year
Europe cheered and returned
to the wreckage of her cities.
No hint of me beneath my mother's
flowered silk, the jaunty
shoulders — that dress lived
for tea dancing and long nights
on the town, officers on leave,
the muted brass of big bands
oozing caramel, as the sea
beyond Manhattan soaked up ash
and the rumbling of the last trains.

By the time I was born, Europe
was patched with old brick
and my father's Navy whites
hung in darkness, our nation quiet
at its borders. Every night at six
this family of four sat
down to dinner and smiled
through white teeth like TV people
while the dog who didn't know better
stalked other dogs in neighbors' yards.

By the time I was born
the schmaltzy music had faded away.
Everyone slept eight hours a night.
I came into the world
without a single memory.

In the Very Beginning

She is too young to talk. Lamplight
wraps her against the falling dusk
as her parents change her diaper
and tease each other by talking to her,
"Isn't he a silly one, isn't she
a goose?" Their laughter is pure water
holding them together and to her
in the moment: this night, the white
clapboard house, their clear blue
and brown eyes, their luminous young bones.
She looks up and tries out her voice
one bubble at a time, fledgling vowels.
The smell of ointment is almost
sharp, not quite medicine, familiar
as their hands, as she drifts
in a warm swell that flows without effort
or boundary. Without source or destination.
Now I think of that one night, the light
and laughter that held us, as a single
jewel — topaz, say, or amber, worn close
to the skin for a time and then lost
or tucked away. I think my parents must have
left that room feeling full of themselves
and of me. That they held each other
in full bloom and woke the next morning
cradled in a sense of bounty so simple it needed
no measure. Like water from a new well.

Ambition

I

More than anything I wished I'd been named Mickey
like my mother's friend with the red convertible
and hair that cupped her head boldly, a bowl
of black feathers. My hair was the brown
of old grass, curly and sad, and it
never moved when I shook my head.
I was afraid of thunder and scrambled eggs
and other children. I was afraid of my bed at night
with no one to talk to. Mickey would tuck up
her feet as my mother handed her a drink
and I'd watch her, feeling a plan stir
behind my eyes like a room taking shape
with the lights off. Once she put down the top
and took me for a ride all my own — then Greenbay Road
was a tunnel of sky and leaves, blue wind
and summer, no waiting in the back seat
while my mother bought milk and cigarettes, no dinner
eaten early in the kitchen, bite by bite
like a job to get done — just both of us
flying, and my future rushing at the windshield.

I I

All through first grade I placed myself
behind the girl with the longest hair to watch
her ponytail, which fell to her waist,
while the teacher read aloud. It followed her

like an angel, full of light, crouching
over her shoulder or nuzzling her back.
I watched until my own neck felt its weight.
That summer I tucked a cream-silk scarf
in my waistband and leapt over gulches,
reared, wheeled at hydrants turned to rocks
and cacti in my path. My tail lingered a moment,
an echo, everywhere I had been.

I I I
Once I learned to skate, winter
became my season. I stayed outside
until dark, gliding and darting,
leaning into the curve of a future.
The night the gold trophy took its place
by my bed, I stayed overnight
at my best friend's house. The trophy waited.
It filled the room with a swelling image
of me, the crowd's cheer, while I fell asleep
a mile away. My throat burned with all the wind
I had swallowed that day, pumping
towards the finish that kept fading like a wish.
Over and over I saw the blue ice crack
at the starting gun, then the first
long turn, and the big girl in racers ahead;
I was neither boy nor girl, a sprite
stroking into pure white, winter's heart.

IV

I think none of us knew when prime rates
and measles and parent-teacher secrets
thickened the air in our house invisibly
as dust, along with dinners to give
and go to, cocktails every evening,
the lawn to keep trim, my brother or me
breaking our parents' sleep
with nightmares we couldn't describe;
when my parents' supple young selves
withdrew, taking with them a laughter
I may only have dreamed; when disappointment
seemed to have blown in from nowhere
like hard weather, and I took it upon myself
to perfect and polish and arrange
words like lovely stones,
to win the young gods back again and again.

Resolve

It's a sudden hue
of feeling. The tint
that softens the edge between
act and dream. Blue as the bay
at noon, the huge
eye through which I swim

once I've stopped looking back.
It's the flow of words after
a moment of doubt — drought
in the throat. It's the slow rain
that fell this morning
on freeways and fields,

not the cold wink of cash, not
the steel or titanium
I thought it was, forged
by a man in goggles wielding fire,
not sword
or bolt out of the blue —

it *is* the blue, the translucent
cup whose accomplice
is gravity. It's the cup's water
born of polar ice and ozone,
the element that washed us
ashore and held us

while our cells felt their
way into marvelous
folds, peninsulas and ridges,
and we stretched,
then opened our eyes, then
tried our legs for the long climb.

Notes on an Island, Wisconsin

I will never be finished with
the shoreline, where fallen trees leaned
or sank to the water, and minnows drifted
in their shadows — or with the dense
pine, birch, and marshgrass
doubled on the lake's still surface,
or the buttery late-afternoon sun,
or the creaking of the woods all night —
every time I look over my shoulder,
wherever I am, clouds move shadow and light
around me like another kind of
water, and waves lick at the wooden
dock my father built and rebuilt. This
was where his boyhood returned to him
each summer as he guided the canoe through
Kentuck channel, or cut a dead birch into logs.
He shook the city loose, drank deep
of the woods and bloomed into his sure self.

I wanted him to love me as a friend.
I wanted to fish with him and help him
fix the boathouse roof, but then
I would open a novel or a magazine
and suddenly find myself adrift, each word
and photo lifting off the page to pull me
beyond the world I knew as a tomboy and a daughter.
Later I would lift a pot from the stove
or unbutton my shirt, and feel the weight

of woman in my limbs, a visitation, a force gathering
not as lust but the moves of an ancient dance.
I would read and dream, my future surfacing
from this nest of water and trees as glimpses
of worldly life — a graceful arm in cashmere
and bangles, a long-stemmed glass
full of amber, a man's lovestruck gaze. . . .

Sometimes the words I read were the tap
of rain on the roof, or the fire snapping in its
great stone bed, but mostly they bloomed
as the sound of the lake, a mantra
against the weathered dock. That lapping
would go on, I knew, long after we left the lake
to itself, fallen leaves floating awhile
then settling, ice growing thick enough
for my grandfather's Percherons to have
walked across, the grey silent months,
the roof and beams of the empty lodge
creaking, aching with snow.

Prayer

When I walk into this desert, a sea
of sand where mineral
waters gave up, the brown
swells don't fill me with praise
for the God I was raised on.
The sand presses into my palm
its story of breakage
and waiting. The slow work of
wind. Silences longer than lifetimes,
pauses. I turn to the sun
and away again, drinking
a little at a time. I trace
a lizard's tracks and think of
the people who first came here,
built fires at night, and drew the next
step of their journey in the sand.
I wash the dust from my mouth
but not the browns and tans
from my inner eye, not the braille
from my palm, not the heat from my skin,
not the dryness that peels off
and gathers again, bits of myself
adrift over the earth's face.

At the Estate Auction

I want a poem the color of these garnets —
a poem full of plush and dark mead,
nights thick with travellers,
rumors from the castle, old wind
stirring new snow, Yule logs
and virgin forest. I want
a poem the color of history

to carry with me like a scrap of
velvet, a poem that could have lined
camphor-scented drawers where our grandmothers'
mothers kept thimbles and tortoiseshell combs —
this one paces and whines at sealed doors.

I was born too late for brooding
and plumes dipped in ink,
too late for hand-sewn lace,
too late for elegant superstition,
too late for humours, and layers
of silk that enfolded a woman's hips
in a whispering darkness —
I was born under a yawning new sky.

I was born into "howdy" and "hurry," vinyl
and lucite, pop-it pearls and earrings that flashed
fake color like a grin full of good teeth
and newsprint in checkout lines
announcing, disproving, amending

final cures for the malaise we rose to
each morning, awash in old yearnings.

If I could spend just one day
in the past — the last day
of the Dark Ages, or the precise
middle of Napoleon's reign — this bland
room that I am, its walls drained
by a single bulb glaring overhead, might be
furnished at last and made liveable —

so I am drawn towards light
in its veiled forms: amber glass,
cranberry glaze, Beaujolais
in leaded crystal, a raw garnet the color
of cognac, a string of garnets like bits
of crushed grape, this cluster of gem-cut garnets
like no color I've ever seen, deeper
than rubies, handed down from some nameless
cousin several times removed
and full of secrets, like fire
when fire was important.

Shadow Dance

A mysterious woman with green eyes
lives behind the trapdoor in my throat.
I can't see her the way I can
see the others sometimes —
the three-year-old lifting clumps of grass
to her face, the ancient one resting
sun-creased eyes along a magenta line
of mountains, and the half-grown
boyish one skimming a field on horseback.
This one — whose veils sculpt the air
when no one is around, who follows
any music along its road
or where there is no road
into any torrent or cave or grove —
is my vanished twin,
drifting like a foetus in her cell

and she sends me off some mornings
dabbed with a dark blue
fragrance whose Oriental
name, all filigree and chimes,
I can't form in my mouth.
Around my house she leaves ivory
and silver boxes small enough
to hold a single charm, a ring,
a folded note, a pinch of incense. Throw pillows
like splashes of paint. Coral-
studded combs I can't make stay

in my hair. Her large eyes and long
beaded earrings weave a light of their own
in the small room where she's had to dance alone

because her father was afraid
and his father before him,
of women who might open themselves
without plan, like a cat's sudden yawn, not
to a man but to a moment,
to the touchable surface of
hammered gold, to tambourines
and woodsmoke, to midnight silk
crushed between the fingers, to blades
of rain or the wind's brisk shoves
and who, walking by a lake
in the last warm days of August, might
peel off their clothes and swim
for hours, or go out alone

on the neon streets just to slip into
an envelope of bass notes and drifting lights,
dance awhile, and come home.
And her mother and her line
of mothers, afraid of the soft hinges
of hips, afraid of letting their shoulders
heave when words failed. They closed
white blouses over the hollows of
collarbone and throat and turned away

from the guttural musings of woodwinds,
turned away from the fragrant
blue arms of the night, this long line
of trapdoor bodies clammed shut. . . .

If I could just go near her some night,
if she would let me near,
if I could sing to her,
if she would sing back,
if I could run my hands along my body
and feel her leap out in a wave
of hair and fluid shoulders, I'd grab her hand
and dance gold and silver streams
through the tight bark and drying leaves,
the dozing limbs, the tree
of our family that branches through us.

Rose Quartz

Flush of fever in spring. The heart's
true color. So much light cresting
makes me write and rewrite
to you as some soft hand in me
reaches out, groping — aargh, why
do I keep all my doors and
windows closed while the desert
fills with the outright perfume of blossoms
I still haven't seen?
The afternoon glazes to caramel
at 80 degrees, and all I want to do
is wander on the mesa, or sit in the blue chair
stroking the cat, or step into the circle
of your arms for a long, slow dance.
Is that why I'm staring into this rocky
pink heart, its hollows and edges softened
by water to resemble the odd froth
that clings to sand, harboring shells of
delicate animals after the tide
has withdrawn? What lies at the heart
of foolishness, the heart offering
itself belly up, or the mind
trying to nudge something
soft, fluid, into even wedges?
The pink of these crystals
is without blemish or darkness,
is simply pink, blooming from stone
broken from deep cave walls.

Onyx

No one has to tell me what I don't have.
I've tried to love others before you.

Now beneath the mind's dark luster, its
vigilance, its layering of words
like tar over the heart, a weakness

has spread. There is palsy and
bleeding, your brow and shoulders
no longer beneath my hand

and nowhere to put this impossible tenderness.

I do not look for relief.

I never knew what it meant to put
both feet into someone else's life
until I saw you staring out of your fine eyes

as though through bars. Until I ran my tongue
along their creases, and tasted
gunfire, chopper wind, tears held back

and I felt I could share anything.

Until your betrayals pulled sound
from me like birthing groans, breaking
like waves into my sleep.

I stand at the edge of wilderness now,
porous with loss. The smell of decay
unfurls like a net and settles

over my shoulders. It pulls gently.
Farther in, there are brushfires
sweeping the ground, and a black wind

roaming everywhere, stirring leaves
and shadow and gold spots of sun,
nothing sleeping, green shoots living off ash.

I have to walk in there with myself now,
the child left to play in the yard
by herself these forty years,

the child who won't take my hand,
the child who never left my side.

Why She Reached

Eve wanted it more than fig
or grape or pear. More
than sweet water.
More than Adam's pavilion
of branches that floated her to sleep

above the ground each night.
More than peace, she wanted
gleam and shadow, the chafing
that would make her dance with
the dark — she wanted the earth

to pull hard at her feet.
The serpent was her own
mind waking, refusing
not to match that bell
that ricocheted through the trees —

the apple throbbing
with juice and trapped
sunlight. Its taut skin
split against her
teeth, the "yes,"

the first hard act
and she savored it while Adam
slept, and God took in
her flex. The light that followed her
like smoke. Then He said: *Now*

you will hold this great
darkness; your body will swell
with all you know. You will
bend to its rotations,
its expulsions,

its nights of no sleep
and your mate will dance
around you in a fury,
his feet seeking hold
in whatever he can borrow.

So she bears it, every
seed and drop of juice,
fills her plate,
bleeds it out, cries out
in labor but not

when his hand strikes her face.
When she sits awhile with
other women, they exchange
glances like a handshake.
They lean into each other,
their voices low bells
and soon they laugh, they
laugh, they lace the air with
trickery and joy, the juice
aged to bite back, hard cider.

Calypso

She is loved in secret, by
one man at a time seeking
cleared ground in the forest
of his life. She glows against
virgin timber, the dense shadows
and riot of ferns that part
before his exploring feet.
In her cave, candlelight
burnishes the walls around
the half of his life
he has not yet lived,
the wild lover rising through
his hands, his voice,
tenderness too, pure lyric, his thoughts
startling him with night gardens

while the walls of his family home
and the legs of his laden table
and the posts that float
his marriage bed
hold the heft of his days. Sheets
and curtains drying
in the wind, then filling
the house with the scent of sun.
Plates in the drainboard,
the pitcher of juice, all of it
witnessed by those who
belong there, passing easily from

room to room, their touch
braided into wood and cloth and china
even as they forget, touch
them again, go out, come home.

Sometimes she wants to leave the island,
its wildness of her making, only to
find a harsh descent down slopes
the sun rarely touches. Rocks
tower there, balanced against
all odds. Sometimes she
presses against them,
longing to walk in her own flesh
down his flat sunlit street
and see him open his door. The rocks
press back. In their deep cracks flowers,
vermillion and lacy white,
thrive in the shade.

is the only one of its kind.
And one of millions.
I look into its face
and feel clouds moving

across my skin. And feel
animals begin a slow
migration inside me. I wait
for words I've never spoken

to arrange themselves, to push
boulders and dead trees aside.
Words from my belly, heart, and bones.

The animals move like lava
over flat land. Their dark fur
is full of silver. *Fox*
I could say, but these animals

are huge. And graceful as bears.
And the light in their fur is
flint, is deer streaking across

an ice field, is hundreds of white
birds rising from black water.
I want to put my arms around them

but I would be hugging air.
I learn to wait in this chair
for one word, then another
to appear like stars that only

seem, to one who doesn't know
the stars, to rise at random
from the dusk as the mountain
glows by itself, then goes out.

Night Trade

This is the way coyote sleeps:
leaving his skin
behind him, all plumage
and stilled breath.
Taking his skinny self
elsewhere, to dart after rabbits
and dream at the moon. Pealing
howls under the moon, shrill gold coins
tossed to other coyotes and gotten back
doubled. Then he lowers his nose
and curls his tail about his paws, smug
as a housecat, as the coins roll
gleaming into the night to scare chickens
and toss ranchers in their bunks.
All night he licks his lips
over this meal of noise,
this gab-feast with cousins posted
like radar stations in the dark.
By day, they disappear, all
thousands of them, leaving the desert
to sunlight and trucks. They go back
to their sleeping hides: one tanned
carefully by a boy with his first gun,
one eaten by moths
in a Dakota trading post,
one tagged with a high price
on Rodeo Drive, and this one

stretched across the foot
of my bed at the watered edge
of desert, where I wake some nights
shivering in gold light and ghost money.

My Father on the Dock

7 A.M.
Mother hasn't awakened,
motorboats haven't troubled
the air, and the lake holds the last
of the night's stillness. Dad sits
by the water reading a thriller
he may have read before,
skimming the action while his thoughts
rise and fall. Sometimes a minnow
breaks the surface.

Soon mother's *Good morning* from the porch,
her *Ten minutes 'til breakfast*, her
random requests, plans, reminders
through the screen, alters the air
the way a new wind brings rain.
Soon Dad rises to oil a motor
or caulk the scow
and resumes the old laments:
his brothers have neglected
the woodpile, he should have bought
more lumber for the boathouse that sags
from six months of snow, the pump
needs parts that aren't made anymore. . . .

I'm reading too, cherishing
this hour when my thoughts are my own
after the privacy of sleep. I'm home

in the desert three weeks later, remembering
our last walk before I left the island — how my
eyes filled each time I looked at the soft
surrounding water and I longed
to be sanctuary, patient as these shores
that cradle the lake in all weather,
for my selves who tried to be loved;
for the pine-needled clearings
and their silence, sweet and smoky
with sap; for my parents who grow
smaller each year, their admonitions
shooting through me like light
from extinguished stars.

A rustling now in the lodge. Water flushes
through the pipes. Dad turns another page
and watches the lake. My eyes fill again
as my thoughts dip into his and touch
a root too buried for me to recognize
at first as his sadness. Maybe it's mine,
since he doesn't have words for what he
doesn't dwell on — maybe he's saying
goodbye, though when he reads this
he'll tell me I guessed wrong.

Then what is it that fills his days
with wood that needs treating?
Rust that needs oil?

Maybe a quiet fear, a humming
too low for him to hear, that he hasn't
done all there was to do when he fished
this shore as a boy and felt
length and breadth gathering in his limbs,
an animal quickness, and time
spread before him from an open hand. . . .
Here in the desert I hear it
clearly, his father's voice
reaching across the water to call him,
eldest son, rising star, home to chores.

Cruising

This morning I take breakfast on deck
where the sun keeps vanishing before
it has warmed through pile lining
to the heart of me, the part of me not
on tour, the veranda where I'd hoped
to sit awhile — sit without shyness.

I shrink into my jacket and look
for the next patch of blue sky.
The clink of china seems
either exotic or sad, and my shipmates
aged beyond all desire
to be beautiful, as though leisure

were a form of gravity.
I'd like to think I will never
be like them, gripping both rails
when disembarking, and wheezing
on the steps of ruins.
I'd like to think the steps of ruins

hold the imprint of my shoe
long after I've gone back to a hot bath,
when moonlight gives marble the sheen
of living skin. I'd like to think
I can hold at bay myself as one of history's
invisible women — that *I* could have

fought until I dropped
for my country — its olive trees,
its oracular voices,
its green and wounded hills.

French

Two pretty children
at the station, disobeying
their mother to play trains
with the luggage, lisped without faltering
through a trellis of syllables,
their words single pearls
I caught and held awhile, my ear
softening to pearl

and even the concierge, hurling
reprimands into the phone
to the dispatcher who forgot
to send my cab, sent sound into the air
like bon-bons cast from fragile
shells at the back of her throat.

In the streets, serious business
clattered by like boots on cobblestone,
or fanned into branches of air released
from any word containing "r,"
or floated from cafes with the sound of spoons
stirring sweetness into coffee's strong bite —

and always, the lilies and tiger mums
and chrysanthemums along the curb,
the windows full of scarves,
the windows full of lamplight, drapery, and fern,
the windows full of frosting and glaze, baguettes

and tangerines, tawny perfumes, meats iced
and fresh as red and white blossoms — the whole

boulevard at dusk glowed like a necklace
while Belgian chocolates
in my mouth bloomed one by one
into *merci . . . oui . . . cuisine . . . chaumière . . .*

and always, the mother river
of language flowing
past me, perfectly clear
and too cold to swim in.

American Flight #549

This time I make myself
think of plumage —
an aqua sound, birdwings
not hammering
but rustling the air,
pushing and pulling, threading it
through a boundary —
not this white noise,
breath of the times I live in.
And me — a citizen of cramped seats
and the roar of heavy machinery
six miles up — I no longer
have the sense to remind myself
I'd explode if dropped from this height
or mind that a whole country
slips beneath me, acres of
roofs and grassblades, landfill,
oil on puddles, secret paths
children have made through
weeds & discarded crates
to remnants of a cellar. What do I
do but keep looking at my watch,
chew ice cubes, and read
the same page again?
While someone's cat slips
from a house filled with talk shows
and the smell of burnt coffee,
its paws leaving fragile

dents in the sand.
While a baby takes itself
by surprise, walking three steps
towards a blue flower.
While a woman in her kitchen
sets out bowls, spoons, yeast, eggs,
a bag of flour, jug of milk,
pushes up her sleeves
and plunges her hands into the past.

Museo de Oro Lima, Peru

This room could have been Pizarro's first dream —
coins, masks, bracelets,
a little universe of gold.
But soon it wasn't enough, all
the Incas brought him,
trusting, their llamas weighted with light —
gold poured through his hands.
The heat of his wanting
melted it down.

So gold became the rumor of itself,
driving armies across the Andes' murderous spine,
the wilderness of having and not having.
My mother thought money
would make her safe.
My father thought money was proof of goodness.
I am terrified of debt
and you, whose father left you nothing, have brought me an
abandoned self

to fill. When we first entered this room
the lights were dimmed.
The treasure had tarnished in its history
of wrong hands. We had not spoken
for days, our silence armor, thickening.
Then the room brightened slowly —
gold dawned around us
mutable, loved, and we
woke to it briefly, unburdened.

Gourd

Baked the color of sand
and fitted with hemp, it holds
rainfall. It is carried over the adobe
land and hung against sand-colored
walls, inside or out, while the sun beats
water to sand, and the sky
thrums overhead, endless
and deep, a great exhalation of breath.
When I run my hand along the once-green
skin, I can feel it breathe. I can
feel sky running through its veins.

When I drink from its heart
and eat the bread baked in the smooth
clay ovens that rise here
like temples, I can taste sunlight
ground against sand-colored rock
and saltwater flaked from dried
oceans, where men and women formed
a ragged line from the Bering Strait
pulled by a god for whom they had no name —
each night along the way must have been
like no other, a grain of rest
inside the dome of firelight.

Here the very fields know how to wait.
They flare green when they can.
They subside and flare green again

the way this brown fruit holds rain
for months in its fortress shell
until a man's or woman's hands
lift it into use, sand-colored hands
with sand in their creases.
They offer water to the land, they
shape the land into bricks and tilt more
water to their faces, containers of silence
warmed to fine leather from looking
at sky, looking down, looking
at sky again.

Feathers

His hands, fair-skinned and well-
fed, thrive on touch-tone buttons
and expensive pens. They send his voice
every day like an arrow into the world of
high finance and favors,
bull's-eye, nine to five.
This morning they find the fit of
shell to gun barrel without a false move
while his eyes travel
skyward, pinning flushed game.

This is the new part: he stoops to pluck
a few feathers from the downed
pheasant, then nests them
in his hunting bag like game itself —
the elegant tail spears
and almond down etched with fine ovals,
etched in the sure strokes
of a calligrapher sitting by
travelling water, surrounded by birds
who pause to dip their bills
and then lift away in a
single sheet, smooth wing singing on air.

The governor sees him kneeling, hands
full of feathers, and is too amazed
even to guffaw. But the eyes say
George, what the hell are you doing?

He looks up, thinking to say,
They're for a friend who asked for them,
but the governor's camouflage cap
has sprouted branches full of fearless
singing birds. And his own eyes
have alighted on a mountaintop softened
by mist, farther east than he has ever been.
A stream lulls itself over the patient stones
as he dips a feather again and again into
rare black ink. He answers, *The slow*
poem I didn't know I was writing
is warming me up. I want to
hold my hands here a while longer.

Amethyst

A deep stone with many streets,
its light holds itself in with
blue, then pours sunlight
over the windowsill. My fingers
run like water over its edges
and I feel a small rose opening, a pulse.

I gave off light like this once, listening
to poems beside a man I hadn't
known long, feeling my thoughts
simply braid into his.
We didn't touch, and later we stopped
writing letters, but that night
a sheath of heat held us, and the light
rising from me for once was muted,
not diamond, or daydream spending itself
in sparks, and it never quite left.
One morning, expecting tartness
and seeds from purple grapes that appeared
along a stranger's fence, I tasted
sunlight. I tasted snowmelt
washed down from rock and pure air.
At times it seems that benevolence
thrives in a small enclosure.

Today the sun turns these grey
mountains gold, dusky pink, then spills shade
over their canyons which deepen

to blue as the light begins to leave.
The bay gelding walks
to the end of his pen and dips his nose into
black water, not drinking, just
splashing it, playing,
making it gleam in the soft dark.

Mauve

I

In their sleep, the men I loved began
my instruction. One spoke a tongue
foreign to me at first
as it must have been to him, a river
of syllables pumped from sleep's
sure heart. By day he spoke
through locked teeth, an old anger,
his words hard as buckshot.
I got out of range by
leaving my body, leaving
in its place a cold blue light
he came to know well; whenever he
flared, my own words sharpened
into metal and good sense.

But at night I opened myself
to that other tongue — I glimpsed
his father taken early by illness
and hidden in the heart's
walled city, while his mother refused
to hold a man's hand again, or laugh
from the center of her body —
I glimpsed the boy cutting a path through
trees and tall grass, then dozing
in a hayloft while horses munched below —

I followed his sounds until they
ran through my head like a song.
He led me to a garden taken over
by thistles, by briars, fragile
and lovely in their frost.

I found myself kneeling there,
a child just big enough to seek
refuge from those who would protect her,
studying my own hand
as though it had just sprung from the ground.

*

The other gathered me
and arranged me across the table
as though I were green and full
of sun. He coaxed me with talk,
with hands, to love my own hands
as different from others', to love
my breasts. My skin grew supple
over the way I was made.
Another me sprang up
like one of my own ribs turning
to blossom. To red fruit.

In his sleep he turned wholly
away. If wakened he curled
around his hands, his back

a shield. I found myself
pinned beneath the ghosts
of women — the longings
and quarrels gathered in his heart
like silt, all that was left
of the light their hands might have
given him at first. I could hear
his breath fill with sand,
with bedrock grown thick —
that's when I knew what had
grown in me had not
grown there.

For a while then, every nightfall
passed something like a hand
over my cheek and made me
grateful to be lowered
gently into the lamplight
of myself until daybreak.
Until thin light sneaked back,
casting the shadow of mountain
over my door and over the fields
behind this house, where all the green
had bled into sand.

Every morning I put on something red
or the clear blue the sky might
or might not offer, and stepped out of my house
as though into a stranger's body.

II

Now I've grown lighter, my skin
sometimes sponge, sometimes
air. Now the nights bring
silence, then sleep.
Sometimes rain. Then dawn
and its simple changes.
I follow them, passing in and out
of my house while the fields' flowering
passes in and out of me.
Sometimes what I'm writing keeps me
dreamily indoors, as poems
turn to dune and river beneath my hand.
Or the telephone lifts me from work
and passes me into other, possible lives:

Esther is dazed from the pull of others'
secrets, from opening and closing
doors of herself to let them pass.
She only half-knows others' dreams
are her first language.
She only half-knows she is
brave. She listens hard
to their stories until she finds
herself at their source —
the sister, the mirror,
the dark saint — then gathers

herself from her jewelled hive of rooms
to greet husband or son or lover
who cracks a secret door in himself
while thinking her his own, his single
blue or white or rose-colored stone.

Susan, who stopped painting for years, now
sleeps at night between an ocean
and the first man she's ever known who doesn't
need to talk. Who doesn't need to
shelter in the tropics of her heart,
its thick roots and tribal mothers.
She picked him for his hands, fluent
with chisel and nails. She picked him for
glancing calmly out the window now and then,
not knowing himself observed.
At first he didn't notice her bottomless eyes.
Now she begins to paint again,
beach glass or shells. Bits of wood
washed a long way, worn smooth, not broken.
Her dreams, she says, have lost their furious colors.

Lightning

The slant of light as in a Vermeer interior
is what I carry from the kitchen of my parents'
first house — the lamp's brownish glow
and the worn linoleum underfoot
the color of bricks. To me at two
the room seemed a kind of passage; hot oil
flew like needles from the frying pan to where
I watched everything come and go
from a high chair, learning
my first moves of flinch and caution.

This was 1949. Forty years later
I wonder what the couple next door
might have longed for — Mr. Fiweiger in his
bald spot and wilting shoulders, his wife
in curls that somehow were no color
and never moved when she walked —
both shrank behind their Venetian blinds before
the '50s even got under way. My young parents
painted and papered, laid new tiles and
built cabinets, busying themselves
around their vague bewilderment,
the future exposed like a newly
paved highway before them.
I practiced turning myself back into
a leaf, a crow, an Indian girl
with a name like water running over rocks.

Our yard's small wilderness
of scrub and ancient leaves halted
at a pine fence. Beyond it, the yellow
"400" shot by twice a day on gleaming rails;
my father would hold me on his shoulders,
clasping my ankles as though he knew I could
fling myself into that wake of flash
and blur. The night the single oak crashed
in our yard, I marvelled at the snap
of heat, whiteness, seared wood and
thunder, a noise like building after building
folding to earth. This is the last
memory I have of living without dread,
as though my body were a moccasin
made from a deer's fluent skin.

What made me wake rigid two years later
in our new house, a summer storm
tearing at my sleep and filling me with
hollows? At each flash I pressed
my palms against my ears and waited
for the sky to break around my head,
my fear a vagabond that finally had found
a place to live — or had it been
waiting inside me, a prisoner
tracing hairline cracks in the walls?

When my first boyfriend took me to watch
fireworks, I surprised us by cowering

beneath the bouquets of light that opened
and opened, exuberant against the charcoal sky.
I felt my heart, my throat, go dry as seared grass
as each explosion shook the air from my lungs.
My hands flew to my ears. I willed myself
to be no more than a single eye,
a shell with no flammable heart inside

and last summer I couldn't swallow as I forced
my car across a bridge in a thunderstorm, feeling
spotlights train on me, playing,
giving me just seconds to make the other side.
I felt myself glow from the inside out
as though stripping down to meet them —

clearly I have died this way before.
I can almost remember the crack, no pain,
just a fist of light as the last of the world
to enter my mind. I can guess the rest —
that I drifted out of my body, feeling
safe again, taking a holiday
from the housing I would cling to
in future storms, each self coming of age
to shrink behind its eyes and ears
as though to hold something in,
keep it from leaving before its time.

Somehow

The thin air of La Paz had been close with
smells — *saltañas*, urine, charcoal,
wet wool. Then we climbed into this brown
sea of a land, its cloud cover,
a few women in jolting pink shawls
driving cows into the wind. *The Altiplano.*
Too high to nourish anything green,
it seemed flung across the top of the Andes
like discarded burlap or canvas.
Snow swam through the air, nothing
to hold it down. Even my head floated.
Then a few sod houses broke the horizon,
inseparable at first from cows.

Their people walked into the weather
without pleasure or dismay, moving
by rote inside their bright wools.
Or they sat like stone in their doorways,
figures carved with ancient tools,
while the rooms behind them seemed to offer
no broth, fire, or rest. How to explain
that they seemed to desire nothing?
They stared through us the way
the very old stare, at some point
only they could see. Their jaws
worked coca leaves over and over,
keeping the tinder inside them barely lit.

We drove to temple ruins nearby, three walls
of vast stones loosened and hauled
from their quarries before the wheel
was invented, then squared
and fitted without releasing light.
They had lost no edge to the grey wind.
They seemed to have swallowed
all substance from the air
and from me. So I understood my life
as accident, my hand raised briefly
against the weight of other lives. My hand
which even the watery dawn passes through.

Lapis Lazuli

How to approach this stone
full of night, this
blue secret? It stares back
aslant, a cat's gold eye
turned dark with dilation.

Once it crouched,
a scarab ringed in gold
over hands that waved peasant
and slave over mounds of cut stone.
Then tombs and temples rose from
the endless sand, proof
of plane and line, heft
and angle, the loosened
tongue of numbers.

It sealed the lids over
Ramses' eyes, the blue rooms
of memory, while his widowed queen
unfastened the cobalt coals from her neck
and tied back her obsidian hair.
It would have glowed
forever in the perfect
darkness of Tutankhamen's tomb
but was passed hand over hand
back to the troubled daylit world

where it makes breath catch
in my throat. Deep sea stone,
calm fist, thought distilled
to a hue too bright or dark to
resemble any soil, grain, granite
or jade, green or browning leaf,
violet or iris, the slate
or sunlit waters of the earth —

its dark beam urges me to
witness what I may or may not
have lived to see — the sun god Ra
winking at midnight. The ancient wind
that sleeps in the pyramid. The translucent
darkness beyond the moon's eye, where invisible
planets flare and subside, light flickering inside them
like messengers with lanterns moving
swiftly through palace rooms.

Aquamarine

A drop of sea, rounded as beachglass
or a tablet of eucalyptus
on the tongue, its color
soothes the eye with the cool
undersides of leaves. This

is the color of sky just before
sunrise, the air in the valley
still freshened from stars.
It's the color of water gulped from the dark
green hose after a ride on the mesa
and the color to ease forgetfulness,
another thirst, giving words
back to a watchful, timid child
who murmured stories late at night.

It's the color of joy
only deeper, perhaps forgiveness,
when the self's right hand
reaches for the left
and holds it, resting. This
is the color that filled my eyes last night
under a three-quarter moon, even though
the pale light flooding the corral
wasn't really the color of sea.
You took my hands, and kept them
long enough to warm them into
a single shape — it shimmered

like a knot of roots lifted
from broken soil. Then you let them go
slowly, as though retracing
that touch for both of us to keep
while the chestnut mare nosed
for grain at our feet, her lips
barely disturbing the rippled sand,
precise as a surgeon's hands
probing a slowed heart.

Sea Opal

Beyond a sea of grass, she could glimpse
the real sea, more a long breath
than a line of blue. It made her touch
her rough sandals to make sure
they held feet she knew.
Sometimes they didn't, and when she
looked up again, the view
made her feel like a guest. Ushered
into a hall of plenty, not
to wines or ritual foods
so much as an absence of want,
by a host who had stepped aside.

Most nights she drifted outdoors
towards the grass, water, and stars
while behind her the village
huddled around one fire, making itself
a boundary. Her husband
slept in the wood house that groaned
in high winds. Sometimes she slept there too.
The night the wars ended at last, she sat
with the others on cleared ground, not singing
but watching the tamed fire until joy burned
through the length of her, a root
of flame singing to the soil.

Each day she passed among the houses
offering simple cures. Salt

air. The scent of grass. Shells
whose chipped sides revealed a fine
scrollwork of spine, a sign
of what the body holds within itself.
She let anyone summon her,
she never stayed long
and made no one wary, including
the man whose house she shared

like the village cats who vanished
through loosened beams when a room filled
with voices and feet, and reappeared
on a nearby sill or doorstep curled
around the fires of themselves.

One Side Writes to the Other:

Miss Homebody, Little Chicken, keep
a light for me by the window.
I need to be in the weather again.
I need to go deeper this time, where no
wall or roof will hold my silence.
I need a lantern strong enough to bring
the moon to eye level, and water enough
to keep me from thinking of water. I need
to crawl into myself as animal, all heartbeat
and heat, when the night thickens
with rain and slowed time.

I need to sit by the fire until I've
felt my way along every wall
of me, the cobwebs and bonepiles
and fertile caves. I need to find
once and for all the high pass that keeps
moving north and sending me back
out of breath and shaking ice from my hair,
sending me back with nothing in my hands
and nothing in my canyon heart, my name
beating against my teeth. Then
I want to dance until my own
feet drumming the ground
weave circle and flame, soil
and blood, a body to hold my dance.

Always you have drawn me home
with candlelight and ginger tea.

You have covered my chapped hands
and said *No one loves you like I do.*
You have coaxed ivy to flow up the sides
of this house and filled the rooms
with flutes, the smell of cinnamon, the pride
of tending what is ours. You have left
books for me everywhere, and said
You're the only one I can talk to.
Still, something keeps falling from the sky
too thickly for words, falls like
buckshot or knives, and I see
it's only water. I am flesh.

I am flesh. This is what makes you
shiver, seeing me set off like before
in nothing but skin and my longing
for touch — for a lover's touch to flare
into nights I can melt down
in my mouth, in my palms, and then place
around you like a circle of polished stones.
You would forget all that, pull your cap
over your ears, and light incense
that smells of English gardens —
I want to let my hair grow wild.

I want to feel the wind tear through it
again, but this time I've packed
whatever in me has waited this long to surface

as pick and fuse to loosen old rock
and a rope that will stretch
anywhere, tied to the end of your chair.

And she answers:

Little soldier, dervish dancer,
puller of roots — I can't see you
growing old. Your future is a winter field,
stripped and brown if I look too hard, so I
pour another cup and fill the house with music
that weaves the air into petals and silks.
Sometimes your face softens, and your eyes
turn away from the window — how I've wanted
you to rest in the bower I've made.

When you pace, the page in my hand
turns to a powder of ink and dried wings.
When your voice grows ragged
with questions, I let our soup grow cold.
When you sit on the porch and stare
for hours at clouds foaming over the mountains
like a wave about to crest, this house
chokes me. I want to fill my lungs and howl.
I fill the saucer beneath each jade plant
and lie down to watch the leaves
fatten and shine.

You go away too much.
You're afraid of stillness
and cannot sleep through the night
but when you come home dazed and chattering,
your hair smelling of sage and your cheek gritty
with tears, when you pull from your pockets bright
peridot and quartz, when you step from your boots
to show me the brave pirouettes shown you
by someone you loved forever
for a while, these rooms
grow golden around you.

Then what I've read or thought all day
fills me with the stories
I've been waiting to love again.
My hand eases the blade through bread, rippling
with candlelight, its skin
suddenly strokable and fine as marble.
I open the garnet wine. Our laughter
starts slowly, then rings from the walls.
Among the apple peels and cheese rinds, sweet
crumbs and crystal, we pass the night
trading secrets and dozing
in one another's arms — you with your flint edges
and musk, me with my omnivorous eyes
that take you in until they darken and shine.

Estrogen

One day I too will be
found, a lightning root
in a sky underground,

marked by whatever the years
will have done — the fur
my hands have stroked, the greens

that pushed through soil
and passed my lips,
the darkness my bones carried

and yes, something
glittering in the champagne
those nights I thought I would live

forever, petal that I was.
The wind wrapped me in a skein of cries.
I aged closer to the ground

and fell in with the weather as she
changed and changed her mind.
My breasts ached.

Then shrank. My bones
thinned to lace. Was this
a departure? Some

would have it so — some
who walk the world with one
blind eye and one empty socket.

Passage

I was born to people who were proud
of being invisible —
German Jews,
blue-eyed Jews,
straight-nosed Jews.
I was taught to disguise my hair
as obedient to gravity
and enter a room without
calling attention away from the petals
floating in Steuben glass, the tweed skirts,
the pleasantries, the slipcovers strangling one another
with good taste, hushed strands of color.

I was taught not to pronounce
the singing, guttural "g"
at the middles and ends of words —
that tribal sound, that homage
to someone else's grandparents
in brassy gold frames,
someone else's third-class
ocean crossing with one canvas suitcase,
someone else's heart tamped and watered over
the dead, the village cobblestones, the dusky fires.

For years I thought I was telling
the truth when I pulled images
from the mind I mistook for my heart
and arranged them in cut-glass poems

like the flowers I was taught to bring my hostess.
I danced with sad men, angry men, distracted men,
matching my step to theirs and thinking myself
graceful. My deserted body mourned, pulling
the muscles taut between my wingbones.
Each morning I jogged past fields of red peppers
and clover in purple flower, and the earth
gently turned her back to me.

Now silver has begun to wander
through my hair like moonlight, or laughter,
or water from a deep spring.
Two horses allow me to think I own them —
to close them in at night and bring them hay.
They guide me over fences and miles
of sandhills I could never cross
alone in this body. They lower their heads
and offer their muzzles and exquisite
ears to my blind hand, teach it to see

and when I ride in the wind and sun
I can feel the bones surface in my face
like ruins. For hours, I watch
the mountains crease and deepen
in the changing light. In the mirror
I see a woman losing her prettiness.
I see an ancestor like no one I know
staring back at me now and then

and I want her to come out.
Now. I want her to fan my hair
each morning with her strong fingers.
I want her to press my ear to the earth.
I want to know what it's like to leave
this body, to fill this body, to lift this body
and set it down again and again by dancing
in one place, by dancing all night in one place
until I find the rock of silence
at the heart of me and warm it with
my own hands — as I write this
I am full of tears, a glacier melting,
the carving trying to be finished.

Running Horse

It's not because the halter in my
hand has any final say
that my black horse, floating
like a planet around me the past
twenty minutes, suddenly gathers himself
from daybreak and air and stops
just inches away, all
the fireworks of first sun caught
in his black tossing head —
he's ready to let gravity
touch his feet and settle him
into mammal again: sweat, hair, hard
lungfuls of air. He slips
his nose through the halter

and I'm caught in the current
between us as though born to it,
a shimmering silence, slow-motion glints
of hand and hide, non-words rising
like bubbles into my mind's washed light
as *wait, listen, touch,* while the sun
pulls itself up another notch
and dissolves the black hole I woke to
this morning alone in my breakable
bones and my memory full of holes,
alone in my other language
forming itself again into lists.

I lead him to the saddle and bridle
and the corral full of jumps. His hide
glows and ripples, volcanic, but his head
doesn't worry the rope, doesn't
lengthen or close the space between us.
He moves on tight springs. The rope
shivers in my hand. My pale body
rises from its crouch over a fire
so deep it may be a dream,
rises in its blanket of fear
and muscle, rises again in its
blood that warms the cold caves.

Calypso, Twilight

The blind stallion, having learned
my braille of leg and hand,
carries me without flinching
at the wind. His back has softened,
an extinct volcano, and my hips
hold me there, settled
by something I no longer
try to name. I am past the years

for bearing. My skin
turns to the work of wind
and salt, as the sun shortens
its arc above my diminished gardens.
I have little use for the silver-
wreathed mirror brought by a lover
who kept finding his way back.

If a wanderer should drift
ashore now and then, spent
and nameless, he will still find
in my eyes a trace of green.
Or blue. Depths in which to rest.
He will still find in my flesh
a firm *yes*, not padding
or pillow, but sinew like his —
from gathering wood for the long nights,
from sending men back to the sea
at first light (they swim strongest then),

from rising alone most mornings
to light that never lies
and the continuous waves.

But this poet who tries to slip
into my skin — she bathes me
in stage light, too bright
yet too soft, scribbling in
her journal. She would have me say,
This is the dance my mothers
and grandmothers might have learned
had they slipped away from
children and set themselves loose
beneath the moon.

I give her back her words, a wish
blown like a kiss as the bloom
leaves her face, and love
leaves a jagged wake behind her.
It would do her little good

to know that lately I slip
like the breeze between the island's
tall rocks. I travel without
green or blue lining my eyes,
without rare flowers
from my garden, and disappear
into rooms filled with smoke, jazz,
the braid and flow of tongues.

I walk through the teeming streets
without desire or dread, the way
the old stallion accepts
the bit and lets himself be guided
among the last of the wild iris,
the shrinking berries —

and sometimes my weakened eyes
feel immense, turning me
inside out, as a young man or woman
appears beside me
speaking slowly at first, as though
cracking the door to a vault
and is surprised at the words,
the rush of words,
the voice full of great birds lifting.

Lent

These nights we wait for
the easing, when Neptune
and Pluto will have
gone their separate ways
again, their gravities
loosened from the seasonal
tug-of-war that plays hell
on each conscience,
that stranglehold of regret
and missed connections.
We ritually banish
ourselves from feasting,
our place in the food chain
no longer recognizable.
We nibble at the edges of
a vague grief and pull
the salt from our tears.
Midnight, and still we hunker
at the table, measuring in ourselves
our ancestors' notion of
goodness by fractions
of an ounce, gold
bought on a gamble —
to save towards what? What
to do but finally
call forth those we have
silenced with our blind
love, our inherited hungers,

the claims of blood ties?
They come to forgive us and move on —
the child, the imp, the merchant
of laughter, the one who
wanted to fly, the one
who dreamed an amazing machine,
the one who stood apart in the photos.
We bury the bones.
The wood in the winter stove,
the kettle singing,
are almost enough now,
almost enough, we whisper into
the last faces, ours,
that wait across the table.

Slow Work through Sand

I wrap her racehorse legs in blue flannel —
the slender bones and tendons that once
strained towards breaking
in a tornado of packed dirt flying,
whips stinging the air, a roaring

in her velvet ears which still
flatten sometimes with remembered wind.
She was bred to run on wariness,
her ancestors' history of flight.
She never drifted under cottonwoods,
sampling the desert's grasses
grown lush or sparse with the flow
of seasons; the snap of a gate, the bell

at her ear, and the earth simply vanished.
The first time I rode her she startled
from under me, all troubled air, leaving me
bruised against the abiding ground.
I rode her in a corral every day
while my ribs healed. My fear softened
with wear, familiar as faded cotton.

She still gathers herself, the old
lightning shooting through her
when a trail stretches
straight before us — all four feet
leave the ground at once, the way I

jolt myself awake at night thinking of
so many days blurred behind me, friends

from whom I've drifted like a lost planet,
works-in-progress abandoned in a drawer,
my parents growing old now, their
insistent questions, my imperfect love. . . .
For a long time she never looked at me,
my sister in caution, peak performer
raised on good grain and indifferent hands.

I pick up her feet and set them down
one by one, a slowed four-beat chant.
I run a brush along the horizon
of her back and comb her long tail
until the strands blend to a dark hush.
I set the saddle lightly as breath

and tighten it one slow notch at a time.
I walk her on a loose rein
until she stops waiting for a spur
and her head lowers to the rhythm of
our hips and shoulders, quail settling
as we pass, the dip and rise of patient
dunes that once were ocean floor.

Taos

West of where I live
as though sometimes walking
in my sleep, the buff-colored
dunes and arroyos deepen to red
until they hold their own
light, and hawks float
slow-motion on currents
of thinned air, taking the long view
which includes me driving
too fast, slowing to a dream,
leaving my car like an empty nest.

The wind pummels the mountains whose ridges
flex, all edge and shadow. I slip
out of my skin, my name and birthdate,
a renegade with no passport
crossing a frontier, not exactly on the run
but vague at the hinges. A swinging gate.
An open window. A husk filling with
hoofbeat, woodsmoke, Spanish
syllables, "esperanza," the wind's hush
and rasp, the cries of quail and chaparral.

I step from my fertile years, wrapped
in a blanket the color of bark
and berries. I step into a beauty
I have dreaded, as the sun

bakes my skin to a map of dried rivers
and my bones dry inside my flesh. I doze
in one of these dwellings whose walls
rise gently from earth, as one by one
the memories like old leaves
fall away — of flight and harvest,
of fire and the long dance.

Then in a window I glimpse
a blue teapot, a row of books, a circle
of lamplight under Tiffany glass —
they jolt me, the way a lace kerchief
in a gaslit saloon must have stunned
the first settlers, their eyes
filled with sky and red canyons
and their wagons nearly bare, the cane chairs
and carved armoires and brass bedsteads strewn
along the westbound track like bodies laid to rest.

This Year Summer Comes like a Catherine Wheel

Even at night we can feel
the heft of absent sun, something
clenched and restless in the air;
wind rakes the valley and
doubles back, displaced by
a shift of elements — tundras
beaten to ash, lava rising
from unspeakable wells — far beyond
the curve of earth we step onto
each morning, thinking ourselves
on a flat surface. Lately
going outside feels like walking into

a fist, and Joel and Karen and Jay
have slipped away from their lives
as though from an island, leaving
us to shift from foot to foot on ground
that suddenly moves. Another friend's son
awakens slowly from a stroke,
his muscles emptied of memory,
a familiar word blooming from his mouth
now and then like a sweet berry.
The days go on and on.
We move slowly and don't know
when we're hungry. Each day breaks
a hundred degrees and we don't want
to be touched, as though we were not
like the beasts that nurse their young,

tip their ears and lean against
one another with closed eyes.

Even a small breeze beats our
skin into sandhills and rising dust.
We drink and sweat and drink.
Diana and Lila and Hattie from college
still look like themselves
after 25 years — the births, the separations,
their parents clutching at their arms in crowds.
Before her tiny wedding this spring
to a man with a grown granddaughter, Hattie
went out for champagne and bought
a white dress that touched the floor.

Night after night the stars look
the same, honed to ice in air
so thin I lose my breath
just to think of it.

Chant

Strong light leaving the sky
drains all ridge, sandhill,
cottonwood, shadow, and dwelling
from the land. Tonight this soothes.
Will and desire have left me soaked
and dazed in sweat, and for once
my eyes want thin gruel, nothing solid.
The dunes deepen in the sun's wake
to bass note. Dying thunder.
Hushed drumskin.

I turn towards that black vibration
and climb, wrapping a new
darkness around me. I leave
a trail that zig-zags without a plan.
I exhale all the lives love
has blown through me —
soothsayer, siren, throned princess,
gypsy with the healing hands,
cistern full of pain,
temptress, pillow, forest
of smells, rumored mistress
of drifters and married men,
virgin on a flying horse — these
disperse over the darkened land.

Piece by piece I call myself back —
skinned thumb. Chapped lips. Innards

growling in their dependable health.
Grey hairs salting the young ones.
Sturdy heart still flexing,
still listening to itself.
Large eyes lined now, nearsighted,
blue with trapped sky. Mouth
full of words. Veins and bones
close to the surface
and something else
I can't name, a small flame

burning in a room that has no windows
below my heart — a room
filled with men and women I've refused
to hold before me, like garments
that might fit, aching to be visible
in their thin skin, their pale or
blistered skin, their ordinary skin. *My kin.*
Tonight I walk into the space they've
taken in my world, and look around
through their saddened eyes.
I feel the land through their shoes,
each sandgrain, hollow, and husk.

I can make out dark mountains
rising against the softer darkness
of the sky like a huge animal
sleeping on its side.

North of here, I'm told,
a canyon holds all the colors
the Indians used to make paintings
of sand — turquoise, white, yellow,
moss green, ochre, charcoal, orange. . . .
If someone looked for me now, they'd
see one clear footprint.
Then another. Pure feeling
feeling its way.

The History of Women   after Jack Gilbert

The history of women sighs
from the iron across the empty sleeves,
the exacting collars,
and edges along the porch rail.
It rises in the arc of a jump rope
then dissolves in a flurry of rhyme,
step on a crack, break your mother's back. . . .
It sends some children home
to the table waiting to
be set for eight, away from the fragrant
dusk, away from the last secret
whispered behind cupped hands.
Still, there are days when a girl
roams alone in her body, humming and
dreaming, a heroine among weeds and wildflowers.
When childhood ends, it is cut at the root
though for a time, the young beauties
spring lightly from buses to offices
without windows, thinking they
will always be pretty
and soon will leave town.
                              Understandable then
that marriage appears to them
as an offer. They mean to
accept. Then they mean to make
the best of it, swimming
in a current that keeps them
in one place, smoothing Oil of Olay

over their useful hands, comforting
their mothers whose sadness
ceases to baffle them.
They wave the last child into
the evening, the first in a string
of crucible nights, and try
not to pace at the window.
Divorce leaves them stunned, supple
as leather, stranded for a time
on a long path towards love.

                                              At times they see beauty
in each other mirrored nowhere in the eyes
of men, or in movies they watch when they
can't sleep. Waiting in a long line
to vote, they sense the shape of themselves
briefly, like ice cubes dropped in a lake,
though the speeches have blurred
to a long hush, waves against sand;
so history drives them inward
with the sound of someone clearing his throat.
Then one day it wakes them up
in the middle of their lives,
in a house that smells of cinnamon
or woodsmoke, surrounded by a small wild yard.
Scrubbed apples drying on a cloth. The sun
just setting, gold over the valley's greens.
Silence everywhere, softening the horizon
and bringing it even closer.

Tonight the Moon

is a sliver of light on a plate —
I swear I can see the whole
plate, the dark side,
the vanished harvest.
Without sadness, I'm thinking this
is how we carry sadness —
not some millstone
shaped like the heart, not a bruise
the size of a continent, but
a residue, a heat
from others' hearts riding the air,
all the breath around us
mixed with diesel, pollen, charcoal,
haze, whatever makes us sneeze
all year around. Gravity
bows and shrinks us
as we age — for a while we
don't notice — but it feels good
to slip outside and let the moon
pluck at some bass note
even if we're taking out the garbage
for the thousandth time.
The sky never changes
and never ends, and this
is unthinkable. Still we try —
our feet grow light
on heavy ground, our eyes
travel up and up, and the hairs

rise on our arms until our skin is an ear
cocked towards every cricket,
every restless leaf, footsteps
along a fenceline miles away —
then we step outside
our lives, even as we step into
our bodies, all four corners,
and ride them home.

1987

Elton Glaser, *Tropical Depressions*

Michael Pettit, *Cardinal Points*

1988

Bill Knott, *Outremer*

Mary Ruefle, *The Adamant*

1989

Conrad Hilberry, *Sorting the Smoke*

Terese Svoboda, *Laughing Africa*

1993

Tom Andrews, *The Hemophiliac's Motorcycle*

Michael Heffernan, *Love's Answer*

John Wood, *In Primary Light*

1994

James McKean, *Tree of Heaven*

Bin Ramke, *Massacre of the Innocents*

Ed Roberson, *Voices Cast Out to Talk Us In*

1995

Ralph Burns, *Swamp Candles*

Maureen Seaton, *Furious Cooking*

1996

Pamela Alexander, *Inland*

Gary Gildner, *The Bunker in the Parsley Fields*

John Wood, *The Gates of the Elect Kingdom*

1997

Brendan Galvin, *Hotel Malabar*

Leslie Ullman, *Slow Work through Sand*